50 FUN-FILLED CROSSWORDS AND WORD SEARCHES BASED ON FAVORITE BOOKS

By Steve Herrmann

SCHOLASTIC
PROFESSIONAL BOOKS

New York • Toronto • London • Auckland • Sydney

For
Deanna, Sierra, Jordan
and all
the great students
at OES
—SH

Cover design by Jaime Lucero and Vincent Ceci
Interior design by Drew Hires

ISBN 0-590-03323-9

TABLE OF CONTENTS

INTRODUCTION

Dear Teachers,

Welcome to *50 Fun-Filled Crosswords and Word Searches Based on Favorite Books!* These puzzles have been created to help in your efforts to bring students and great literature together. The puzzles are not only meaningful, interesting, and applicable—they're fun too!

Here are a few highlights you'll discover as you take a moment to look through the book.

- The titles are arranged alphabetically, making the book easy to use.

- The crossword puzzles focus on plot, theme, setting, and characters, so they're great for reinforcing comprehension.

- The word search vocabulary puzzles include key words from the books and identify the part of speech of each word.

- The suggested discussion questions are open-ended specifically to encourage higher-level thinking.

- Answers to the crossword puzzles and word search vocabulary puzzles appear in the back of the book.

As a teacher, I use these crossword and word search puzzles to supplement the spirited discussions my students and I have as we read these classic books. The puzzles are a great way for students to check their understanding of the novels and to aid you in assessing their progress.

I hope you and your students enjoy these puzzles as much as my students and I have. Happy reading!

Name _____

BANNER IN THE SKY

ACROSS

1. An "old" disabled man with a heart of gold and a lot of pride (2 words)

3. He died on the Citadel because he would not leave another man in danger.

7. The author of this great book! (3 words)

10. Josef Matt reached the base of it.

13. He has an unconquerable spirit, which helped him make it to the top. (2 words)

14. Rudi's hometown.

15. Rudi's uncle, and a great climber. (2 words)

DOWN

2. Rudi's job at the hotel.

4. Saxo's home-town

5. It now flies atop the summit of the Citadel. (2 words)

6. One of Rudi's nicknames: Klaus often called him _____-_____.

8. A young boy whose dream it is to reach the summit of the Citadel. In a way, the Citadel is his mountain.

9. The proud boaster of Broli. Rudi saved his life.

11. Rudi's mother, and widow of the great guide Josef Matt. (2 words)

12. Rudi worked at the ____-____ Hotel.

13. Josef Matt's shirt could be seen on its summit.

5

BANNER IN THE SKY

S	A	Z	T	R	E	G	R	R	B	F	M	C	M	M
E	I	G	O	C	F	W	E	P	F	Z	O	K	D	J
N	A	M	I	D	H	C	D	A	D	M	Z	K	X	H
E	E	S	U	L	I	I	T	R	M	P	G	N	Q	H
R	Q	S	W	L	E	S	A	I	Z	M	D	S	B	K
Y	U	K	P	J	T	Z	G	B	I	P	N	G	G	
Y	W	P	X	L	A	A	Y	V	W	R	U	S	L	R
I	A	P	A	H	P	K	N	Y	O	N	O	X	R	I
H	J	U	P	A	C	X	Z	E	R	U	J	A	O	A
R	U	A	H	H	N	T	J	K	O	U	D	B	M	P
D	H	S	Y	F	K	Z	E	J	Z	U	O	W	Q	S
F	I	O	X	B	C	R	I	A	A	L	S	T	O	E
M	B	M	A	R	E	A	P	T	U	A	L	C	E	D
N	Y	X	P	Z	I	S	D	N	E	C	S	E	D	D
M	A	N	E	U	V	E	R	P	Y	Z	M	S	B	N

Directions:

Fill in each blank space below using the vocabulary words in the box. Then find the words in the word search puzzle.

detour	agile	despair	commit	haphazard
mishap	descend	simultaneous	maneuver	staff

- stick or pole used as a support (noun) _____
- to promise or pledge (verb) _____
- at the same time (adj.) _____
- unlucky accident (noun) _____
- route used when the main one is out; a roundabout way (noun) _____
- to go or come down from a high place to a lower one (verb) _____
- moving quickly and easily; nimble (adj.) _____
- skillful plan or movement (noun) _____
- dreadful feeling that nothing good can happen; no hope (noun) _____
- by chance, not planned, or random (adj.) _____

Name _____

THE BEST CHRISTMAS PAGEANT EVER

ACROSS

1. Imogene smoked one in the bathroom.
3. He was Joseph in the Christmas pageant.
6. The author of this very funny book. (2 words)
8. She was always Mary in the pageant, until the Herdmans came! (2 words)
14. The Herdmans burned this down, and got free doughnuts.
15. This wise man forgot the myrrh.
16. It was his fault the Herdmans showed up at church.

DOWN

2. She was the angel of the Lord.
4. This book is all about a Christmas _____, and much more.
5. The Herdmans brought this to the pageant. They didn't take it back.
7. They were the highlight of the pageant, in the end.
9. She was Mary in the Christmas pageant.
10. The wise man who almost dropped the ham.
11. Towards the end of the pageant, Imogene did this.
12. One of the wise men.
13. People believed the Herdman's cat was really a _____.

THE BEST CHRISTMAS PAGEANT EVER

K	R	E	H	E	A	R	S	A	L	L	G	A	A	R
V	C	N	Q	X	C	E	M	U	L	K	M	X	P	K
O	Z	I	O	Y	S	R	X	T	F	M	N	E	M	R
L	S	D	P	I	I	M	F	T	N	S	N	Y	A	H
U	U	C	R	E	T	Z	W	R	A	I	Q	O	J	A
N	Y	P	I	O	C	A	E	Z	T	Q	N	O	K	A
T	N	O	K	C	S	I	G	E	S	I	X	P	V	I
E	A	N	U	S	G	Y	N	E	K	X	M	C	W	T
E	M	O	Q	M	E	T	P	H	R	X	C	K	X	T
R	R	Z	P	M	I	A	I	H	F	G	M	C	P	E
U	I	M	K	A	G	C	H	Q	O	A	N	L	W	S
I	A	J	R	E	P	F	Q	R	N	A	T	O	Y	N
T	H	Y	A	P	M	J	H	L	C	P	D	C	C	I
S	C	N	T	O	N	R	I	N	E	V	U	O	S	O
B	T	A	P	P	L	A	U	S	E	T	V	V	J	P

Directions:

Fill in each blank space below using the vocabulary words in the box. Then find the words in the word search puzzle.

souvenir	penitentiary	pageant	chairman	congregation
applause	rehearsal	volunteer	ice pick	poinsettia

- person who chooses to serve (noun) _____
- an object given or kept for remembrance; a keepsake (noun) _____
- approval shown by clapping the hands (noun) _____
- plant often used during Christmas as a decoration (noun) _____
- very sharp tool used to chip blocks of ice (noun) _____
- public entertainment, such as a show or parade (noun) _____
- performance of a play or concert for practice (noun) _____
- prison for criminals (noun) _____
- person in charge of a meeting or head of a group (noun) _____
- group of people gathered together (noun) _____

Name _____

BUNNICULA

ACROSS
1. They have fangs, and suck blood or, in this case, juices.
4. The dog.
6. It makes vampires immobile (and smells too)!
7. After Bunnicula got to them, they were white.
10. Bunnicula sucked these out of different kinds of vegetables.
13. Harold loved to eat chocolate _____.
14. Mrs. Monroe's occupation.

DOWN
2. Harold's last name.
3. Bunnicula didn't have teeth, but these.
5. He didn't find Bunnicula, but he was at the movies.
8. He found Bunnicula.
9. The title of this very interesting book.
11. The cat.
12. Chester tried to pound one into Bunnicula's heart.

9

BUNNICULA

F	U	E	Y	F	N	O	I	T	A	P	U	C	C	O
Z	U	C	C	H	I	N	I	P	O	E	Q	N	A	E
S	A	U	N	T	E	R	I	G	F	J	N	T	N	P
T	C	G	H	J	Q	P	F	P	D	O	P	D	X	P
J	R	L	W	C	C	T	P	C	S	I	O	W	I	A
M	J	A	C	L	Q	N	G	I	R	P	O	R	O	Q
Q	O	E	U	L	F	B	N	C	V	F	V	D	U	Q
M	E	A	Y	M	W	U	S	S	U	F	C	C	S	R
L	V	G	K	Z	A	U	O	C	O	Y	J	O	V	L
Y	G	V	O	F	N	T	D	R	U	Z	O	P	K	A
G	R	S	F	A	W	C	I	R	B	C	O	C	B	U
U	M	S	M	Z	P	P	M	Z	O	O	E	W	Y	T
W	Q	K	H	R	I	S	S	N	E	O	R	V	V	C
L	W	J	D	Z	Y	Y	D	Q	I	D	P	H	Q	A
H	I	D	E	O	U	S	A	I	J	C	L	Y	D	F

Directions:

Fill in each blank space below using the vocabulary words in the box. Then find the words in the word search puzzle.

droopy	manuscript	occupation	factual	unison
anxious	traumatized	saunter	zucchini	hideous

- feeling uneasy, troubled, or worried (adj.) _____
- work or employment someone does to earn a living (noun) _____
- kind of dark-green squash shaped like a cucumber (noun) _____
- hanging down (adj.) _____
- very ugly, frightful, or horrible (adj.) _____
- to walk along slowly and happily; stroll (verb) _____
- to be shocked (verb) _____
- book or other material written by hand or typed (noun) _____
- true or certain (adj.) _____
- agreement; together (noun) _____

Name _____

THE CASTLE IN THE ATTIC

ACROSS

4. William's guard while he was in the castle.
6. The author of this great book! (2 words)
8. This magical word caused a person to turn into lead.
10. William's best friend.
12. When forced to look into it, one was faced with all of his or her weaknesses and misdeeds.
13. Of all the people mentioned, he probably learned the most during this exciting experience!
15. William helped him win back his kingdom. (2 words)
16. Sir Simon's horse.
17. Sir Simon's nickname.

DOWN

1. The boy whom William met when he came out of the forest.
2. When William's father built this for the castle, William was surprised.
3. William was very good at this. After all, it helped him defeat Alastor!
5. A magic word, causing people to shrink.
7. She was William's nanny, and very good friend. (2 words)
9. The Silver Knight's old nurse.
11. The terrible wizard who misled Sir Simon's father.
14. William's last name.

THE CASTLE IN THE ATTIC

N	Y	P	F	L	S	X	K	R	G	B	S	G	H	G
N	E	Q	H	C	N	C	N	N	U	G	Y	R	D	R
C	O	K	V	V	M	P	I	R	V	D	D	Q	T	O
N	O	L	O	B	O	R	E	G	X	B	O	M	H	T
W	H	U	Y	T	P	A	E	S	X	W	S	R	O	E
V	M	L	R	S	U	R	Y	A	E	B	T	N	F	S
T	V	W	D	T	I	Z	E	K	B	Q	Q	O	Y	Q
S	A	N	K	U	Y	F	E	G	G	I	A	I	R	U
N	A	Q	Q	Q	U	A	O	S	U	S	H	L	L	E
H	R	S	D	A	W	M	R	Y	I	W	I	L	A	L
B	Y	E	G	L	G	T	Q	D	Z	Z	K	A	V	T
F	G	P	X	P	N	N	Z	U	I	N	C	T	I	R
R	J	C	E	S	T	D	W	U	E	S	E	S	H	D
C	Q	N	D	P	E	J	X	Q	G	G	T	R	C	S
E	D	U	I	W	K	C	I	S	E	M	O	H	F	G

Directions:

Fill in each blank space below using the vocabulary words in the box. Then find the words in the word search puzzle.

homesick	bureau	chivalry	courtyard	token
handspring	squire	stallion	frenzy	grotesque

- longing to be home (adj.) _____
- odd or unnatural in shape, appearance, or manner (adj.) _____
- qualities of bravery, honor, courtesy, and fairness (noun) _____
- young man who serves a knight (noun) _____
- condition of madness or excitement (noun) _____
- full-grown male horse (noun) _____
- chest of drawers for clothes; a dresser (noun) _____
- space enclosed by walls, in or near a large building (noun) _____
- piece of metal used for a special purpose; a symbol (noun) _____
- where a person lands on the hands and then flips to the feet (noun) _____

Name _____

DANNY THE CHAMPION OF THE WORLD

ACROSS

1. Doc's last name.
4. Danny's father broke his _____.
5. Person who tried to protect the pheasants from poachers.
7. In the end, the pheasants deposited their filthy _____ all over Mr. Hazell's car!
9. Mr. Hazell's fancy car. (2 words)
12. Danny had a marvelous one.
14. He's the champion of the world!
15. Danny is the champion of this! (2 words)
16. The author of this and many other spectacular books! (2 words)

DOWN

2. Danny and his father lived in a gypsy _____.
3. Danny's father made his living as a _____.
6. The setting for this story.
8. It appears as though every person in town poached them!
9. Before trying new poaching methods on pheasants, you first try the method on _____.
10. When you soak them, they get plump and juicy.
11. Danny's father never, never, never broke them.
13. He owned the wood where Danny and his father poached pheasants. (Hint: His last name only.)

Name _____

DANNY THE CHAMPION OF THE WORLD

P	J	E	X	V	C	W	G	N	I	H	C	A	O	P
Q	H	R	U	B	B	I	S	H	T	Q	N	V	P	L
R	U	E	M	U	E	K	C	V	L	I	Y	J	E	R
N	W	I	A	W	T	B	T	L	I	R	A	N	I	S
B	B	W	R	S	V	K	I	W	T	U	L	J	P	S
W	X	B	F	K	A	O	N	K	L	F	Y	A	M	U
O	R	O	A	W	D	N	L	K	R	Y	R	Y	B	L
E	C	N	X	L	T	E	T	H	B	K	R	E	K	K
Y	A	O	U	K	U	W	I	E	Y	O	G	K	S	B
F	R	Z	I	V	B	I	J	F	T	P	R	C	Y	O
F	Q	U	V	D	Q	R	P	A	I	M	Q	U	M	Q
U	F	I	I	O	I	H	V	X	U	R	A	U	O	K
R	Q	I	Y	D	O	A	K	R	Q	C	T	N	L	J
C	S	Q	N	N	L	Y	M	F	A	T	I	E	I	U
S	C	C	Y	J	B	T	Z	Q	X	K	M	X	P	A

Directions:

Fill in each blank space below using the vocabulary words in the box. Then find the words in the word search puzzle.

scruffy	phony	pheasant	rubbish	sparky
quirk	lavatory	poaching	mania	petrified

- large game bird with brightly covered feathers (noun) _____
- unusual or unreasonable fondness; great excitement (noun) _____
- trespassing on another's land to hunt or fish (noun) _____
- enthusiastic or determined (adj.) _____
- worthless or useless stuff; waste; trash (noun) _____
- peculiar or different way of acting (noun) _____
- not well groomed; dirty (adj.) _____
- bathroom area where you can wash up; toilet (noun) _____
- fake; pretender; not genuine (adj.) _____
- to be paralyzed with fear, horror, or surprise (verb) _____

DEAR MR. HENSHAW

ACROSS

5. The author of this and many other great books!
7. Leigh's mom.
8. Bill, Leigh's dad, had a hard time expressing them.
9. Mr. Henshaw told Leigh that if he really wanted to be an author he should read, look, listen, think, and _____.
11. Leigh's dad often told him to keep his _____ clean.
13. School janitor who was nice to Leigh. (2 words)

DOWN

1. Leigh asked her if she know Boyd Henshaw. (2 words)
2. Who knows, perhaps someday Leigh may become a famous _____.
3. Leigh's parents were _____.
4. Leigh and his mother lived here.
5. Bandit wore a red one around his neck.
6. Leigh wrote many of these to Mr. Henshaw.
7. Leigh's dog (although it didn't stay with him).
10. Leigh's father drove a really, really big one.
12. Leigh built one for his lunchbox.

DEAR MR. HENSHAW

M	E	R	I	G	V	U	E	W	E	U	F	A	C	F
U	I	S	N	D	O	P	J	P	T	L	F	Y	G	R
P	B	L	U	J	J	V	U	I	W	Q	S	N	J	J
S	M	G	D	M	B	G	W	R	Z	C	V	J	T	R
E	U	T	V	E	A	D	Y	G	G	E	V	F	E	B
T	W	H	Q	Q	W	E	Y	K	V	A	U	T	K	D
C	W	E	J	S	I	A	M	A	I	R	A	E	H	Z
N	H	W	C	Q	F	D	B	O	D	C	T	J	A	M
J	K	K	T	Q	A	L	B	I	S	A	N	V	R	C
M	C	M	Q	G	K	P	A	R	C	E	Y	X	H	L
R	F	Y	V	M	L	R	I	I	P	C	N	C	D	T
E	M	O	P	N	Y	P	L	U	X	Y	I	O	C	K
H	G	P	Y	T	O	P	W	D	H	K	A	M	L	A
T	G	K	W	F	U	E	H	V	K	M	T	W	O	B
X	T	O	F	D	U	J	D	Q	W	M	F	U	W	C

Directions:

Fill in each blank space below using the vocabulary words in the box. Then find the words in the word search puzzle.

amuse	upset	duplicate	comic	rig
diary	lonesome	cater	ripoff	mildew

- an exact copy (noun) _____
- slang word for an eighteen-wheel truck (noun) _____
- fungus that appears on things when they're damp (noun) _____
- book for recording what's happened or your thoughts (noun) _____
- having a lonely feeling (adj.) _____
- to cause to laugh or smile or feel cheerful (verb) _____
- funny book with pictures (noun) _____
- to cheat or take advantage of (verb) _____
- to provide food, supplies, and sometimes service (verb) _____
- to disturb the order of (verb) _____

DUNC BREAKS THE RECORD

ACROSS

4. Because Dunc and Amos were _____, Milt gave them the bar of gold.

5. Milt's full name, first and last.

7. Amos was crazy about her. (Hint: Her first and last names.)

10. This is just one book in this very popular adventure series.

11. Bat droppings.

12. It's all Amos and Dunc were wearing when they were kidnapped.

14. Amos played this game with Milt.

DOWN

1. Amos and Dunc were attacked by thousands of them!

2. Dunc and Amos set three of them! (2 words)

3. The author of this and many, many other exceptional books.

6. The kind of wind Dunc and Amos were caught in.

8. Dunc and Amos flew in one for quite a while! (2 words)

9. The only thing Melissa ever gave Amos: _____-___-____.

13. Dunc's best friend. (Hint: His first and last names.)

DUNC BREAKS THE RECORD

W	N	A	I	E	T	F	A	R	D	P	U	M	G	W
G	P	P	C	M	O	I	O	Y	A	S	I	L	D	I
L	U	M	X	J	B	K	B	L	J	D	I	W	E	L
F	A	A	N	G	Z	E	A	A	D	D	A	K	S	D
L	W	U	N	Y	Z	Z	L	A	E	L	R	W	C	E
I	B	G	N	O	K	P	Y	R	A	E	R	S	E	R
K	B	H	E	C	O	K	K	H	R	S	X	J	N	N
H	N	P	C	N	H	C	T	D	V	D	Y	I	T	E
G	I	D	C	Q	E	R	P	F	X	Q	P	W	S	S
Z	E	J	I	O	E	R	E	U	O	X	Z	N	X	S
U	W	M	T	D	Y	W	O	Z	P	C	W	A	U	S
Y	O	U	N	A	T	N	U	S	E	O	Z	X	Z	C
L	I	A	F	A	G	J	C	T	I	E	P	F	N	S
M	E	D	L	Y	O	B	J	T	P	T	R	M	D	F
N	T	O	A	O	U	T	G	L	G	X	Y	B	I	W

Directions:

Fill in each blank space below using the vocabulary words in the box. Then find the words in the word search puzzle.

glider	launch	breeze	updraft	guano
descent	wilderness	Neanderthal	generosity	midday

- uncultivated or desolate region with no people living in it (noun) _____
- bat droppings (noun) _____
- noon (noun) _____
- upward movement of air or wind (noun) _____
- aircraft without motor that relies on air currents to fly (noun) _____
- willingness to share with others; unselfishness (noun) _____
- light, gentle wind (noun) _____
- the act of coming down from a higher to a lower place (noun) _____
- to push out or put forth into the air (verb) _____
- belonging to a group of prehistoric people (adj.) _____

Name _____

HANG TOUGH, PAUL MATHER

ACROSS

1. Paul's sport.
3. Paul's doctor, and good friend. (2 words)
4. One of Paul's nicknames for his brother.
5. Paul beat the Ace Appliance team, sitting in one of these.
8. Paul was born to do this.
9. Paul pitched two innings to this team, though he shouldn't have. (2 words)
12. City in Michigan where this story takes place.
13. Coach of the Wilson Dairy team. (2 words)
15. Paul only lost one game. It wasn't because of his pitching, but this.
16. The author of this great book. (2 words)

DOWN

1. Paul's nurse.
2. The team captain of the Wilson Dairy team, and Paul's good friend.
4. Umps say this to begin a game. (2 words)
6. Paul is telling his story from here.
7. Though life threw Paul a curveball, he kept _____.
10. Paul has this disease.
11. Paul's team. (2 words)
14. Dr. Kinsella's nickname for Paul.

19

HANG TOUGH, PAUL MATHER

T	F	S	A	O	B	Q	K	E	M	E	R	P	U	S
G	O	B	H	H	X	Z	C	W	O	L	X	W	P	S
L	R	F	C	R	R	P	Q	G	N	L	T	R	Y	J
P	F	L	F	L	I	C	I	A	L	V	O	Q	U	Z
D	E	E	E	U	O	E	O	C	R	N	T	M	I	H
Z	I	F	P	M	O	B	K	L	O	F	P	F	D	K
E	T	F	X	K	W	E	Z	U	L	I	Q	A	C	B
T	L	N	T	U	K	Q	N	A	R	I	I	L	Z	D
A	B	Y	T	H	J	C	I	E	R	N	S	D	H	G
U	F	E	T	N	E	M	C	O	I	G	G	I	Q	F
T	W	Q	Q	M	E	M	R	Y	Z	V	I	I	O	O
C	Q	G	E	K	A	T	R	A	L	C	L	I	E	N
N	B	N	U	L	S	E	P	D	E	I	P	E	M	R
U	T	E	Q	C	U	U	S	Z	I	C	D	B	Q	A
P	L	R	L	A	E	F	F	D	N	O	M	A	I	D

Directions:

Fill in each blank space below using the vocabulary words in the box. Then find the words in the word search puzzle.

pronouncement	punctuate	leukemia	shriek	supreme
diamond	collision	umpire	reign	forfeit

- rare, usually fatal disease (noun) _____
- to break or interrupt at intervals (verb) _____
- hitting or striking violently together; a crash (noun) _____
- person who rules on the plays in the game (noun) _____
- infield of a baseball field or the whole playing field (noun) _____
- to lose or have to give up (verb) _____
- formal statement or declaration of an opinion or decision (noun) _____
- to rule, have power, or be in charge (verb) _____
- highest in rank or authority; the greatest (adj.) _____
- loud, sharp, shrill cry (noun) _____

Name _____

HARRIET THE SPY

ACROSS

3. Harriet's home room teacher. (2 words)
6. The author of this extraordinary book.
7. Harriet was one for the school Christmas pageant!
8. It may be wise to not bother people on this day of the week!
10. Sport's dad was one! Harriet wants to become one.
12. Harriet's nurse, nanny, and good, good friend. (2 words)
14. Harriet wrote in one, almost non-stop!
15. The scientist.
16. People called Peter The Boy With The _____ Socks.

DOWN

1. Sport's real first name.
2. Harriet played this game with Sport, Janie, and Dr. Wagner.
3. Harriet's least favorite subject.
4. Harriet's age.
5. Harriet rode in this contraption to spy on Mrs. Plumber.
9. Another name for a CPA.
11. Harriet ate this kind of sandwich every single day!
13. Ole Golly said that people who love their work love _____.

HARRIET THE SPY

Y	Y	H	L	B	L	B	W	O	E	V	A	I	V	D
I	R	T	D	Y	Z	I	A	U	G	S	T	E	I	R
S	M	N	E	F	S	E	B	H	O	V	T	G	E	U
K	T	M	T	I	E	E	W	B	L	U	N	T	Q	T
Y	S	X	E	I	X	T	Z	R	O	I	I	Z	T	A
L	R	T	Y	N	M	N	M	R	T	A	W	H	S	D
I	B	M	D	J	S	A	A	Y	W	O	Z	S	O	C
G	N	P	N	F	S	E	G	B	W	B	N	V	U	J
H	U	T	G	O	H	E	M	I	E	A	H	N	T	F
T	I	A	A	E	D	U	I	B	N	H	Z	U	W	K
T	L	N	L	I	D	V	Z	S	C	A	T	W	E	P
K	Z	H	T	F	A	J	U	D	D	U	T	A	E	M
L	L	O	X	G	C	N	B	X	N	M	P	I	O	J
E	R	C	V	K	Z	G	X	I	B	K	X	T	O	L
N	H	S	W	C	Y	L	S	U	O	I	B	U	D	N

Directions:

Fill in each blank space below using the vocabulary words in the box. Then find the words in the word search puzzle.

anxiety	dubiously	route	editor	dumbwaiter
immense	loathe	imagination	dignity	skylight

- fixed, regular course of travel (noun) _____
- very large; huge; vast (adj.) _____
- box that can be pulled up or down a shaft to send food (noun) _____
- uneasy thought or fear about what may happen; worried (noun) _____
- window in a roof or ceiling (noun) _____
- creation of the mind; people thinking things not real (noun) _____
- head of a department of a newspaper or magazine (noun) _____
- to feel a strong dislike and disgust for; abhor; hate (verb) _____
- filled with or being in doubt; uncertainly (adv.) _____
- proud and self-respecting character or manner (noun) _____

Name _____

HATCHET

ACROSS

1. Brian ate _____ eggs.
5. The animal that hurt Brian's leg.
7. The author of this outstanding Newbery Honor book.
9. It was Brian's best friend while alone in the wilderness.
11. It took "just" this to solve problems.
13. Brian named it "Brushpile One."
14. Birds which Brian learned to kill easily. They were great to eat!
15. Brian's father lived here.
16. Brian was cooking this when he was rescued.

DOWN

2. Brian's age during his incredible ordeal.
3. Brian was attacked by a _____. It nearly killed him.
4. Brian spent _____ days in the wilderness by the lake.
6. It was the key to fire.
7. Brian ate them and paid the price afterwards! (2 words)
8. A destructive, whirling column of air.
10. Brian's English teacher.
12. Brian "shared" his turtle eggs with this animal.

Name _____

HATCHET

F	K	B	V	M	R	E	D	U	T	I	T	L	A	J
C	O	P	I	L	O	T	I	B	Q	P	Y	S	O	C
J	O	U	R	N	A	L	V	F	D	U	T	L	E	O
K	C	A	J	N	W	F	J	J	A	E	T	V	L	C
T	Q	E	J	A	L	J	Z	P	L	J	R	I	A	K
I	R	P	B	D	V	R	N	W	I	E	A	C	W	P
D	E	A	W	V	A	U	I	I	D	J	S	I	R	I
L	B	L	N	K	A	T	E	I	Z	S	E	O	G	T
X	H	I	Y	S	M	I	S	V	C	N	Y	U	T	F
W	M	T	Q	N	M	N	G	V	E	G	A	S	N	K
X	O	D	N	A	O	I	Q	S	G	Y	Y	J	A	O
E	L	N	R	C	C	Q	T	U	U	Y	I	P	M	P
W	A	W	E	P	X	T	A	T	I	G	K	U	R	I
Z	Y	R	O	L	N	S	B	X	E	L	D	V	O	V
X	P	D	D	L	V	C	F	I	A	R	L	E	D	L

Directions:

Fill in each blank space below using the vocabulary words in the box. Then find the words in the word search puzzle.

altitude	copilot	jolt	cockpit	vicious
quill	dormant	journal	reconsider	transmitter

- not active; quiet (adj.) _____
- stiff, sharp hair or spine, like the end of a feather (noun) _____
- equipment for sending out signals (noun) _____
- fierce; unpleasant; evil; wicked (adj.) _____
- to think again (verb) _____
- to jar or shake up (verb) _____
- daily record of what a person thinks, feels, or notices (noun) _____
- height above the earth's surface (noun) _____
- assistant or second pilot in an aircraft (noun) _____
- place in an airplane where the pilot sits (noun) _____

HOW TO EAT FRIED WORMS

ACROSS

2. The first worm came from a pile of this.

4. When Alan asked Billy if he would eat this, Billy declined.

5. The number of worms Billy had to eat.

9. The author of this extraordinary "read-it-before-lunch" book. (2 words)

11. The first worm Billy ate looked like one of these.

12. Billy's mother.

13. This worm was eaten raw.

15. Alan put Billy here, so he couldn't eat the fifteenth worm.

DOWN

1. Billy's mother made him a Whizbang Worm _____.

2. Billy wanted to win the contest so he could buy one of these.

3. Billy's father.

5. The bet was for this much.

6. He ate fifteen worms!

7. Billy's friend. He helped Billy throughout the whole experience.

8. The doctor's name.

10. He bet Billy he couldn't eat fifteen worms.

14. He brought Billy the last worm.

HOW TO EAT FRIED WORMS

A	N	X	I	O	U	S	J	N	F	D	G	Q	M	A
B	L	U	B	B	E	R	V	W	K	T	H	U	P	P
G	R	I	M	A	C	E	R	O	A	K	S	T	X	O
O	R	J	H	J	A	K	Z	B	D	S	N	Q	R	L
P	B	L	T	G	G	B	Q	G	E	I	M	D	X	O
C	L	S	Q	Z	S	V	F	D	G	G	F	E	G	G
B	Y	H	E	D	B	R	H	H	P	T	A	R	X	I
C	H	C	W	Q	C	C	T	T	C	V	W	R	H	Z
N	V	V	G	M	U	C	A	C	Q	V	K	E	S	E
P	B	Y	A	F	R	I	M	D	Q	F	Z	T	I	K
X	C	J	U	A	E	L	O	A	E	B	U	A	P	B
T	K	B	W	V	S	N	C	U	N	K	C	E	E	I
I	K	L	G	K	M	H	W	P	S	U	D	H	E	F
Z	E	K	R	X	E	I	C	Q	Q	Y	R	C	H	Q
R	U	U	C	D	X	J	H	M	Q	I	J	E	S	H

Directions:

Fill in each blank space below using the vocabulary words in the box. Then find the words in the word search puzzle.

mussed	blubber	manure	anxious	obsequious
grimace	apologize	sheepish	cheater	night crawler

- any large earthworm that crawls on ground at night (noun) _____
- made untidy or messy (verb) _____
- fat of whales; to weep noisily (noun; verb) _____
- someone who deceives, tricks, or isn't honest (noun) _____
- dung or refuse from stables (noun) _____
- to say you are sorry (verb) _____
- to be polite or obedient, because you may gain something (adj.) _____
- uneasy because of thoughts or fears of what may happen (adj.) _____
- awkwardly bashful or embarrassed (adj.) _____
- to make a face showing disgust or disapproval (verb) _____

THE INDIAN IN THE CUPBOARD

ACROSS

4. Little Bear took this many scalps.
5. The Indian's name. (2 words)
7. Omri's best friend.
8. The cowboy's name.
9. The cowboy's nickname.
10. The author of *The Indian in the Cupboard*. (3 words)
12. Perhaps this was the reason the cupboard worked the way it did.
13. Omri bought the plastic toys here.
14. The main character in the story.
15. Little Bear shot Boone with one.

DOWN

1. The only adult to see Little Bear and Boone.
2. Patrick's brother hid the cupboard here.
3. Little Bear belonged to this Indian group.
6. It changed the plastic toys into real people.
9. The Indian girl's name.
10. Little Bear lived in one.
11. Where Patrick found the cupboard.
12. Squash, beans, and this are considered "the three sisters."

Name _____

THE INDIAN IN THE CUPBOARD

M	T	L	O	N	G	H	O	U	S	E	K	K	O	V
N	A	N	T	R	O	U	S	E	R	S	G	I	U	M
P	R	G	U	U	U	O	U	R	C	L	M	B	L	S
U	O	F	N	O	T	N	S	T	Y	G	G	L	C	H
Z	M	A	V	I	M	N	J	R	S	T	F	A	D	J
S	K	D	W	Y	F	S	E	F	X	U	L	N	T	O
U	S	O	Q	J	Y	I	M	S	P	A	D	D	B	
O	U	T	B	C	P	L	R	D	I	H	Z	T	J	J
I	O	J	W	P	F	R	E	C	D	R	E	G	E	Y
C	L	N	A	X	H	P	H	N	K	D	E	E	S	I
I	E	Y	U	U	P	A	O	L	P	A	L	P	N	K
P	V	J	A	S	O	C	D	O	F	B	T	Z	X	C
S	R	U	D	T	E	L	F	K	N	Y	B	R	X	E
U	A	F	I	S	N	T	L	N	I	S	G	K	P	O
S	M	C	P	F	A	Y	C	O	O	R	K	K	A	F

Directions:

Fill in each blank space below using the vocabulary words in the box. Then find the words in the word search puzzle.

secondhand	trousers	marvelous	scalp	experiment
magnify	suspicious	dismount	longhouse	chaotic

- not new, already used by someone else (adj.) _____
- questionable; distrustful (adj.) _____
- very confused or disordered (adj.) _____
- skin on the top and back of the head (noun) _____
- to make look larger than the real size; to increase the size (verb) _____
- another name for pants (noun) _____
- large, rectangular dwelling of certain Indians (noun) _____
- to get off a horse or bicycle (verb) _____
- causing wonder; extraordinary (adj.) _____
- to try or test to find something out (verb) _____

Name _____

ISLAND OF THE BLUE DOLPHINS

ACROSS

2. San Nicolas is said to be not too far off the coast of this state.

3. They led Karana back to the island after she attempted to leave. They are an omen of good luck.

8. Ramo's made-up name. He made it up when he pronounced himself the new king and ruler of Ghalas-at.

10. We know the main character by her real name, Karana. Her made-up name was ___-___-___-___. (Hint: It was the name she told Ulape in the beginning.)

13. Karana befriended him, though he once belonged to the Aleuts. His death left Karana deeply saddened.

14. Karana's father, and chief of the people of Ghalas-at.

15. He killed Karana's father and lied to her people. (2 words)

DOWN

1. The real name for the Island of the Blue Dolphins.

3. Another name for an octopus.

4. Karana befriended and cared for a seal. She named her _____.

5. Karana and her people lived in _____-_____ at one time.

6. The Aleut girl who became good friends with Karana.

7. Karana tried to leave the island in a _____ but was forced to return.

9. He was attacked and killed by the wild dogs.

11. They killed many of Karana's people.

12. Ramo's sister. She lived alone the island for many years.

ISLAND OF THE BLUE DOLPHINS

R	W	W	B	V	E	H	T	V	X	N	A	L	C	T
Z	J	L	Z	L	N	V	E	E	B	V	R	O	A	S
O	B	E	S	H	R	D	O	A	B	N	R	L	I	A
Q	J	Y	G	D	P	B	W	C	D	M	E	D	U	U
G	S	X	D	M	I	R	E	K	O	L	M	T	Y	Y
A	F	L	E	D	E	B	O	R	K	P	A	M	W	U
M	M	L	B	A	I	S	A	Y	U	D	E	N	J	R
C	B	G	N	J	Z	N	Q	J	T	E	P	L	D	M
Y	W	Y	N	Z	T	C	C	R	E	V	F	S	T	O
E	E	Q	L	D	J	O	L	U	N	C	X	J	W	D
L	W	O	A	Y	Y	B	H	L	A	W	M	Y	U	L
R	H	W	F	Q	W	Y	X	L	V	E	G	X	K	E
A	N	R	A	V	I	N	E	E	B	A	J	K	E	S
P	Y	A	Y	Q	E	Q	Y	T	I	N	E	R	E	S
C	O	N	C	E	A	L	N	K	P	Z	W	W	V	U

Directions:

Fill in each blank space below using the vocabulary words in the box. Then find the words in the word search puzzle.

serenity	cormorant	conceal	parley	pelt
cove	headland	ravine	seldom	dawn

- peace and quiet; calmness (noun) _____
- small, sheltered bay; inlet on the shore (noun) _____
- to put out of sight; hide (verb) _____
- beginning of the day; first light of the east (noun) _____
- long, deep, narrow valley eroded by running water (noun) _____
- point of land jutting out into the water (noun) _____
- to discuss matters or things, especially with an enemy (verb) _____
- large sea bird (noun) _____
- skin of a fur-bearing animal before it is tanned (noun) _____
- rarely or not often (adv.) _____

Name _____

JAMES AND THE GIANT PEACH

ACROSS

5. Believe it or not, every bit of soil has passed through its body within the past few years.
6. The author of this book. (2 words)
8. He plays beautiful music! He now plays for the New York Symphony Orchestra.
10. James' parents were killed by an angry one.
11. Though she's very useful, not many people like her.
12. Went into business with spider, making ropes for tightwalkers.
14. He had lots of feet! He said 100, but he really only had 42.
15. You'll find her in the torch held up by the Statue of Liberty.

DOWN

1. His parents were killed.
2. James and his friends traveled in a "giant" _____.
3. They caused James and his friends a lot of trouble! (Hint: They often "rain" on our parades.)
4. They had a hard time eating the peach, though they certainly tried!
7. The big journey for James and his friends ended in this city.
9. Enormously fat, very short, and mean. And, by the way, now rather flat.
11. Tall, lean, and very mean. And, by the way, now rather flat.
13. Farmers buy sackfuls! This creature was mighty proud of that!

Name _____

JAMES AND THE GIANT PEACH

I	T	B	J	U	A	X	E	C	N	A	S	I	U	N
M	P	E	C	U	L	I	A	R	W	T	E	G	P	P
T	A	V	J	O	T	X	K	Z	T	E	K	R	R	I
P	E	S	B	C	G	M	K	G	D	M	A	Q	E	N
I	O	N	S	O	N	H	A	N	I	L	J	W	C	N
C	J	A	I	I	K	I	E	Z	L	S	M	E	I	A
M	A	A	X	S	V	D	W	E	P	A	K	O	O	C
C	K	P	X	G	U	E	C	E	I	I	G	J	U	L
D	J	E	K	Y	N	O	C	H	Q	Z	R	E	S	E
S	T	V	B	S	M	T	M	R	C	O	B	E	A	H
C	W	L	P	U	A	I	G	I	A	E	E	G	Q	V
I	Q	V	R	C	F	R	A	R	L	S	J	O	S	C
I	Z	K	L	W	R	D	P	G	C	N	C	Y	J	E
Y	Y	E	Z	H	Z	I	W	C	H	Y	S	A	U	P
R	S	U	H	H	T	E	H	G	H	Y	R	Y	L	K

Directions:

Fill in each blank space below using the vocabulary words in the box. Then find the words in the word search puzzle.

nuisance	cellar	peculiar	spectacles	precious
murky	rascal	massive	limousine	pinnacle

- large and luxurious car (noun) _____
- highest point (noun) _____
- thing or person that annoys, offends, or is disagreeable (noun) _____
- eyeglasses (noun) _____
- underground room; usually under a house or building (noun) _____
- dark and gloomy (adj.) _____
- having great value; worth much (adj.) _____
- mischievous person (noun) _____
- strange; odd; unusual (adj.) _____
- big and heavy; large and solid; bulky (adj.) _____

THE LION, THE WITCH AND THE WARDROBE

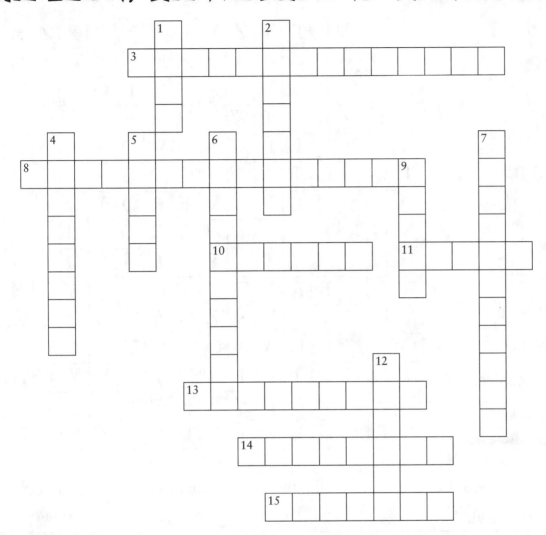

ACROSS

3. Once Edmund tasted it, he wanted more, and more, and more, and... (2 words)
8. He gave the children, and Mr. and Mrs. Beaver, some very special gifts. (2 words)
10. He betrayed the others, but returned in the end.
11. He gave his life for Edmund, but came back to life.
13. As rulers in Narnia, the children chased it. Then, they found their way back into the real world. (2 words)
14. Lucy met him on her first visit into Narnia. (2 words)
15. This book is an example of _____.

DOWN

1. She was the first to enter Narnia.
2. The exceptional author of this book.
4. The children were able to get into Narnia through it.
5. The oldest boy.
6. The wicked ruler of Narnia, until she was defeated.
7. The Professor's housekeeper. (2 words)
9. The oldest girl.
12. The secret land the children visited through the wardrobe.

THE LION, THE WITCH AND THE WARDROBE

A	P	H	K	R	T	Z	V	L	V	N	P	P	Z	H
I	G	A	L	G	K	A	P	M	M	H	X	W	S	G
R	Y	S	R	M	E	U	A	G	J	P	O	I	A	W
R	F	Q	L	C	W	W	R	H	B	M	L	T	C	A
A	H	P	Q	L	E	M	T	O	W	O	S	F	P	R
I	Q	X	C	T	A	L	E	G	O	D	A	W	E	D
D	Q	Y	H	B	F	B	V	F	R	Q	W	W	K	R
S	G	K	E	Z	E	F	H	A	E	T	C	U	L	O
U	N	V	M	Z	J	S	Y	T	L	G	P	G	E	B
W	O	R	B	A	L	T	U	W	O	O	J	A	B	E
Y	H	Z	Y	E	R	N	Z	G	A	M	G	P	Q	O
O	C	M	D	U	A	S	Q	E	G	U	J	I	L	J
J	C	G	O	J	L	I	S	H	M	W	V	Y	C	D
P	E	C	M	Q	L	H	B	A	W	Y	E	X	A	H
R	E	P	U	L	S	I	V	E	N	D	K	S	P	G

Directions:

Fill in each blank space below using the vocabulary words in the box. Then find the words in the word search puzzle.

air raid	wardrobe	mothball	foolish	parcel
courtyard	logic	repulsive	sledge	stag

- space enclosed by walls, in or near a large building (noun) _____
- causing strong dislike (adj.) _____
- heavy sled or sleigh, usually pulled by large animals (noun) _____
- piece of furniture, like a closet, for hanging clothes (noun) _____
- attack by enemy aircraft, especially bombers (noun) _____
- without good sense; unwise; silly (adj.) _____
- full-grown male deer (noun) _____
- small camphor ball, used to keep moths away from clothes (noun) _____
- bundle of things wrapped together; package (noun) _____
- sound sense of reasoning (noun) _____

MATILDA

ACROSS

2. Matilda used it on her father's hat. Ouch!

5. Matilda's school. Its name certainly matched the headmistress' personality! (2 words)

10. Matilda's best friend who was her own age.

12. Matilda's parents and brother moved to this country, in a real hurry!

15. The main character of this book. (By the way, it's also the title.)

16. The hammer-throwin' headmistress of Crunchem Hall—until Matilda was finished with her!

DOWN

1. Mr. Wormwood sold them.

3. Slang for television.

4. Miss Honey's father's first name.

6. Lavender put one in the headmistress' water!

7. The 10-year-old, boil-nosed warrior of Crunchem Hall.

8. Matilda's favorite teacher, and new mother.

9. Matilda's favorite teacher's first name.

11. Matilda's mother always played this game.

13. Matilda put a _____ in the chimney. Her family thought it was a robber or a ghost!

14. The massive headmistress' first name.

MATILDA

I	G	N	O	R	A	N	T	A	F	T	L	R	R	T
J	E	A	L	O	U	S	P	J	B	Z	V	J	N	F
O	B	V	I	O	U	S	E	I	X	K	K	A	E	K
S	T	U	N	N	E	D	B	J	N	J	I	G	M	M
T	K	W	E	J	M	C	C	U	E	L	N	U	F	D
S	A	Z	M	D	M	S	H	U	L	A	H	I	K	E
C	B	D	U	F	N	H	D	I	M	U	N	J	X	H
K	T	D	O	A	A	I	R	O	G	N	I	B	H	B
I	F	V	T	R	S	B	N	H	A	T	X	G	H	T
L	L	R	G	M	A	A	M	A	X	A	V	K	S	I
E	C	Z	E	M	L	T	A	D	F	U	C	G	I	R
F	W	Z	Y	B	L	U	I	C	B	C	J	V	B	P
V	E	C	E	P	Q	B	H	O	L	V	R	P	B	L
N	Z	L	Z	A	C	Y	A	S	N	W	Q	O	U	U
P	E	R	M	A	N	E	N	T	Z	G	N	X	R	C

Directions:

Fill in each blank space below using the vocabulary words in the box. Then find the words in the word search puzzle.

adoration	stunned	ignorant	permanent	jealous
rubbish	brilliant	culprit	bingo	obvious

- game where players cover numbers on cards (noun) _____
- having a dislike or fear of rivals; filled with envy (adj.) _____
- act of admiring (noun) _____
- easily seen or understood; very plain or clear (adj.) _____
- to be bewildered or overwhelmed (verb) _____
- person guilty of a fault or crime; offender (noun) _____
- worthless or useless; waste or trash (noun) _____
- knowing little or nothing; not aware of (adj.) _____
- having great ability; splendid or magnficent (adj.) _____
- intended to last; not just for a short time (adj.) _____

Name _____

MR. POPPER'S PENGUINS

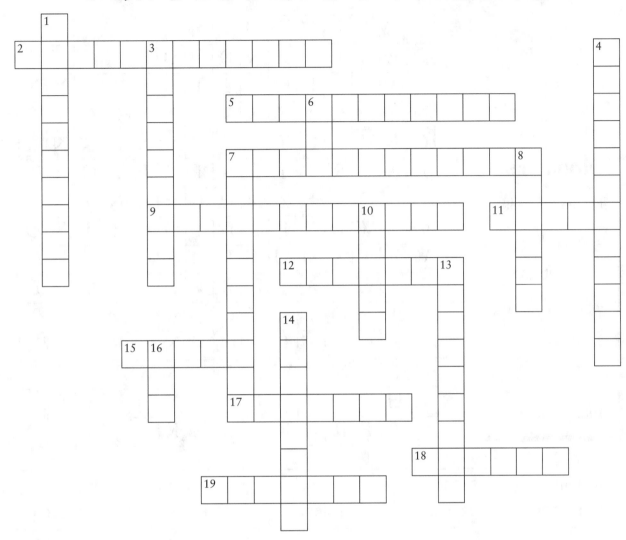

ACROSS

2. Where Captain Cook first lived at the Poppers.

5. The first penguin's name.

7. This act was performing at the Regal Theater.

9. He gave Mr. Popper the penguins.

11. The second penguin's name.

12. Mr. Popper's favorite kind of bird!

15. The penguins would do this when the "Merry Widow Waltz" was played.

17. A penguin's nest.

18. Mrs. Popper played the piano with them on.

19. The authors' last name.

DOWN

1. Poppers _____ Penguins.

3. The last name of the owner of Palace Theater.

4. Mr. Popper's occupation.

6. Greta had this many children.

7. The Poppers lived in this town.

8. One of the penguins' favorite foods.

10. Mr. Popper went to the _____ Theater instead of the Royal Theater.

13. The penguins were going to this place when the book ended.

14. The film company that wanted to use the penguins in movies.

16. The floor of the Popper's house was covered with it!

MR. POPPER'S PENGUINS

P	C	A	L	C	I	M	I	N	E	G	L	O	F	S
B	E	S	P	L	E	N	D	I	D	R	M	G	R	E
U	I	N	C	E	H	E	I	T	H	P	T	X	Y	N
N	E	H	G	I	Z	J	V	B	L	F	E	G	Y	S
G	F	W	R	U	T	G	E	G	V	X	A	R	N	A
A	A	X	R	I	I	E	R	T	P	P	E	O	R	T
L	G	O	Y	Y	Z	N	H	E	D	K	N	J	Y	I
O	L	W	E	W	E	P	D	T	O	U	Z	J	X	O
W	F	T	S	M	M	I	L	O	A	G	P	X	K	N
Z	I	C	K	A	T	A	R	V	S	P	K	C	O	D
A	J	S	O	I	R	Y	G	R	B	I	M	Q	S	T
W	K	C	O	I	P	J	Q	V	N	L	R	Y	Y	X
O	F	N	M	G	W	H	E	A	A	S	T	B	S	N
C	H	D	V	M	V	B	E	O	N	H	U	V	E	N
Q	A	F	R	C	R	Y	B	N	K	L	J	T	A	D

Directions:

Fill in each blank space below using the vocabulary words in the box. Then find the words in the word search puzzle.

calcimine	expedition	bungalow	admiral	debris
sympathetic	penguin	splendid	rookery	sensation

- colony where birds or animals are crowded together (noun) _____
- web-footed sea bird from Antarctica and other cold places (noun) _____
- journey or voyage for some special purpose (noun) _____
- small one-story house (noun) _____
- solution used to wash walls and ceilings (noun) _____
- brilliant or glorious; magnificent; grand (adj.) _____
- having or showing kind feelings toward others (adj.) _____
- strong or excited feeling (noun) _____
- scattered fragments; ruins; rubbish (noun) _____
- naval officer having the highest rank (noun) _____

Name _____

MY SIDE OF THE MOUNTAIN

ACROSS

4. Sam helped a little old lady pick them. He considered them his!
6. The place Sam often visited to find out important information.
9. They kept Sam company while living alone on the mountain. You might say they were his best friends.
10. Sam made his home inside a huge hemlock _____.
11. Sam left this city, well, just because he wanted to.
12. Sam's last name.
13. The king's—and Sam's—provider.
14. He really let Sam have it after Sam caught him in a trap. (2 words)

DOWN

1. The mountains Sam called home.
2. The nearby town where Sam often visited the library.
3. The librarian. (2 words)
5. Frightful would often catch this type of animal. (Hint: they hop and often have fluffy tails.)
7. A lost English teacher. He became very good friends with Sam.
8. They were very interested in Sam's story, at least for a while.

Name _____

MY SIDE OF THE MOUNTAIN

C	F	A	L	C	O	N	E	R	T	Y	Q	V	O	R
P	A	A	M	A	T	E	U	R	F	A	G	X	I	V
H	O	R	C	J	U	R	N	N	O	S	I	N	E	V
E	B	T	E	I	K	G	S	N	A	F	O	D	K	O
A	J	B	N	F	H	U	H	G	U	M	Y	K	R	T
S	Q	Y	A	E	R	K	H	I	T	H	D	G	N	B
A	Q	E	Q	T	D	E	W	U	S	K	A	E	U	Q
N	L	I	F	T	W	I	E	T	R	N	D	Q	X	A
T	K	O	P	J	E	Z	F	F	S	N	G	I	H	H
M	C	P	X	Q	C	Z	S	N	E	S	U	S	M	G
V	O	U	Z	X	B	A	V	P	O	E	I	H	O	L
P	L	M	U	A	K	V	E	H	Q	C	G	J	H	L
W	M	E	L	Z	D	D	M	X	I	Z	T	R	O	O
L	E	T	U	N	N	I	G	Q	F	D	E	I	O	M
A	H	K	N	I	F	P	U	E	Q	S	M	W	X	G

Directions:

Fill in each blank space below using the vocabulary words in the box. Then find the words in the word search puzzle.

independent	confident	carefree	gorge	organs
venison	hemlock	pheasant	amateur	falconer

- deer meat (noun) _____
- type of large game bird (noun) _____
- person who does something for pleasure, not for money (noun) _____
- person who breeds, trains, or hunts with falcons (noun) _____
- thinking for oneself; not influenced by others (adj.) _____
- deep, narrow valley that is rocky and usually has a stream (noun) _____
- without worry; happy (adj.) _____
- parts of animals, like the eyes, stomach, heart, and lungs (noun) _____
- tree with drooping branches; its bark is used in tanning (noun) _____
- firmly believing; certain or sure (adj.) _____

Name _____

SARAH, PLAIN AND TALL

ACROSS

3. Papa didn't do this anymore—until Sarah arrived.

4. Sarah missed the _____ most of all.

5. Sarah's neighbor. She helped Sarah feel at home.

7. Mr. Witting placed one of these in the paper, for a new wife.

10. Maggie gave Sarah plants for her _____.

12. The young boy in this story.

13. Sarah did this when she saw one of the dead lambs.

DOWN

1. Sarah's was yellow.

2. Sarah was this. (3 words)

4. Sarah's cat.

6. She became Mrs. Witting.

8. Sarah taught the kids how to do this in the cow pond!

9. Sarah came from this state.

11. *Sarah, Plain and Tall* won this special award.

SARAH, PLAIN AND TALL

H	T	E	G	K	N	R	R	A	I	L	I	M	A	F
O	O	X	S	F	W	O	U	I	P	R	L	Z	T	H
V	B	M	E	Z	V	S	I	N	T	H	P	F	M	D
Y	W	U	E	N	E	M	K	Q	T	Y	C	B	R	E
E	M	Z	T	L	O	B	Z	J	D	K	G	K	K	Q
M	P	T	W	W	Y	T	L	G	N	U	W	S	N	W
M	Q	W	G	G	O	P	S	I	Q	A	U	O	N	K
W	Y	Q	V	L	B	U	F	H	U	D	I	R	X	R
S	Q	D	B	N	M	G	D	Q	T	L	N	B	S	O
E	U	W	L	F	N	Z	S	T	E	R	T	B	M	F
I	O	Y	H	C	U	O	E	D	M	C	A	U	U	H
L	Q	R	D	G	F	N	N	Y	A	H	O	E	P	C
L	H	L	G	C	N	A	D	T	O	Y	R	L	H	T
U	E	E	O	O	D	W	E	I	J	I	B	D	T	I
G	V	F	B	Y	U	S	M	K	Y	V	B	H	O	P

Directions:

Fill in each blank space below using the vocabulary words in the box. Then find the words in the word search puzzle.

hearthstone	familiar	homely	colt	pitchfork
bonnet	gullies	dandelion	squawk	dusk

- covering for the head, usually tied under the chin (noun) _____
- young male horse (noun) _____
- stone in front of a fireplace in a home (noun) _____
- time just before dark (noun) _____
- to make a loud, harsh sound (verb) _____
- simple, everyday, plain (adj.) _____
- tool for lifting and throwing hay (noun) _____
- ditches made by heavy rains or running water (noun) _____
- well-known; common (adj.) _____
- bright yellow flower that blooms in spring (noun) _____

Name _____

SHILOH

ACROSS

2. He fixed up Shiloh
4. Mean dog-abuser.
6. Marty's sister.
9. Marty had a serious _____, but he worked hard to solve it.
11. Last name of this talented author.
13. Marty tried to keep Shiloh a _____, but his parents found out.
14. Marty wanted to go to this type of school—maybe he'll be able to.
15. Judd Travers gave Marty this in the end. Marty was very surprised.

DOWN

1. Someone like Judd who kills out of season.
3. The Prestons lived just outside this city.
5. The old schoolhouse.
6. Marty's best person friend.
7. Marty's dad. (2 words)
8. Shiloh was this type of dog.
10. Shiloh and the Baker's shepherd got in one.
12. He loved Shiloh, and was willing to do anything to make him his own.

SHILOH

G	S	R	E	F	Q	X	I	R	E	P	M	I	H	W
V	L	W	U	F	L	R	K	W	W	Z	S	S	O	U
P	O	Z	Q	O	R	E	Q	I	B	F	K	V	G	V
R	B	T	Y	P	T	A	F	X	Q	T	V	Q	F	K
J	B	R	O	J	Z	E	N	R	A	E	G	S	O	N
E	E	A	A	D	X	B	D	K	T	V	V	C	Y	Z
E	R	A	E	E	K	F	S	E	F	P	C	H	I	A
T	D	T	N	I	R	L	R	S	I	U	Y	A	T	Q
N	T	G	I	U	E	I	K	C	R	H	R	T	Q	O
A	M	A	W	P	N	I	K	J	Z	X	N	T	M	E
R	X	T	A	A	L	U	Q	B	D	Y	N	W	E	Y
A	E	W	R	L	P	U	Y	S	M	P	C	D	A	R
U	C	I	E	V	A	K	Y	Y	L	V	V	G	A	D
G	A	T	W	M	K	T	M	E	Z	Y	D	D	P	J
N	V	O	D	Y	S	U	O	I	C	I	P	S	U	S

Directions:

Fill in each blank space below using the vocabulary words in the box. Then find the words in the word search puzzle.

detour	whimper	veterinarian	guarantee	skillet
slobber	pickup	frankfurter	suspicious	dawn

- smoked sausage or beef (noun)   _____
- doctor or surgeon who treats animals (noun)   _____
- small truck with an open back, used for light hauling (noun)   _____
- beginning of day (noun)   _____
- road taken when main road can't be used (noun)   _____
- pan with a long handle, used for frying (noun)   _____
- to have saliva or drool running out of the mouth (verb)   _____
- promise or pledge (noun)   _____
- to make a low, sad cry (verb)   _____
- causing one to suspect; not trust (adj.)   _____

Name _____

THE SIGN OF THE BEAVER

ACROSS

1. Matt's father gave him this as a gift.
7. The author of this great book. (3 words)
10. Bows are made of the branches from this tree.
11. The Indian word meaning "good for nothing."
12. Saknis gave this gift to Matt.
14. Attean and Matt killed one together.
16. Every Indian boy needed a _____ to become a man.
17. Attean was a member of this clan.

DOWN

1. The Indian word "medabe" means _____ _____.
2. Ben stole it from Matt.
3. Attean lived in one.
4. The main character in *The Sign of the Beaver*.
5. Matt lived in this state.
6. Matt attempted to teach Attean how to _____.
8. Matt's family was late in arriving because of this illness.
9. A trap used to catch small animals.
12. Attean's grandfather.
13. The Indian word for "tomorrow."
15. Matt's Indian friend.

Name _____

THE SIGN OF THE BEAVER

I	Y	N	T	I	V	S	N	I	S	A	C	C	O	M
D	L	M	J	C	S	X	Y	R	A	T	I	L	O	S
F	V	X	F	E	F	V	F	J	M	R	O	K	X	M
U	G	G	S	B	G	I	R	G	D	K	C	R	A	U
T	M	G	Y	E	R	T	D	T	J	W	H	W	T	X
I	H	J	A	T	R	E	H	X	N	C	G	L	C	D
K	S	Z	Z	H	O	A	E	W	N	I	D	O	E	B
E	E	F	L	D	P	Q	N	C	W	R	N	U	R	R
D	R	F	Z	Z	A	E	M	S	H	F	J	Z	I	M
R	I	A	X	P	V	U	Y	A	I	C	S	G	V	A
A	A	I	N	Y	J	D	D	D	X	F	L	Y	K	M
W	P	O	C	Q	E	V	E	R	D	Z	L	O	C	S
K	S	A	X	G	I	N	P	D	C	Y	A	I	T	U
W	E	Q	F	C	T	E	N	E	D	K	A	T	N	H
A	D	T	E	Q	V	C	U	X	Q	H	D	M	U	T

Directions:

Fill in each blank space below using the vocabulary words in the box. Then find the words in the word search puzzle.

advice	flint	confident	solitary	breechcloth
awkward	moccasins	despair	snare	wigwam

- dome-shaped hut once used by eastern Native Americans (noun) _____
- loincloth (noun) _____
- soft leather shoes (noun) _____
- very hard stone that sparks when struck with steel (noun) _____
- noose or trap for catching small animals and birds (noun) _____
- living or being alone (adj.) _____
- suggestion; opinion about what should be done (noun) _____
- clumsy; not graceful or skillful (adj.) _____
- believing; certain; sure (adj.) _____
- to lose hope (verb) _____

Name _____

STRIDER

ACROSS

3. Leigh asked Geneva to do this on their first "date."

4. Leigh's rich friend.

6. Leigh referred to his house as one, before he called it a cottage.

7. Leigh's track coach.

8. The author of *Strider* and *Dear Mr. Henshaw*.

11. Geneva had hair the color of this type of butterfly.

12. Leigh's best friend—and the title of this book.

13. This book is this boy's diary. (2 words)

DOWN

1. Leigh really enjoyed doing this with Strider, so he went out for track, and was very successful.

2. The cute red-headed girl.

5. Leigh had dual custody of Strider with him.

6. When Geneva cut her hair, she gave Leigh a strand, so he could knit one.

9. At times, Leigh was _____, but Strider helped him out!

10. Leigh taught Strider to _____.

11. Landlady.

STRIDER

Y	N	E	I	Q	X	C	X	Q	W	G	R	P	C	N
I	D	A	L	E	G	U	X	L	U	D	N	O	T	I
M	H	O	G	G	N	D	H	I	C	R	M	E	Y	C
M	Z	O	T	Q	D	Q	T	P	L	P	X	Q	E	K
O	M	Z	E	S	G	E	Q	K	U	M	I	S	Y	N
R	T	C	R	U	U	C	A	L	L	O	A	H	M	A
T	Z	F	R	T	T	C	S	D	G	P	I	C	Y	M
A	N	M	B	K	V	O	C	S	L	Q	G	F	G	E
L	M	H	G	Y	R	O	R	U	U	I	A	H	V	I
I	H	K	P	Y	N	U	Y	Y	R	O	N	P	V	T
M	L	P	I	S	B	D	B	F	B	Z	I	E	K	Y
M	O	V	U	B	F	E	C	V	L	W	S	X	J	F
R	I	L	I	E	Q	V	T	W	C	D	M	B	N	C
N	T	S	S	N	R	G	C	Z	B	U	U	X	I	A
O	H	L	A	N	D	L	A	D	Y	D	C	R	N	D

Directions:

Fill in each blank space below using the vocabulary words in the box. Then find the words in the word search puzzle.

nag	rubbish	deadline	anxious	landlady
custody	compulsory	consult	immortal	nickname

- familiar, often shorter, form of a person's name (noun) _____
- to irritate, scold, or annoy (verb) _____
- latest possible time to do something (noun) _____
- woman who owns buildings that she rents to others (noun) _____
- required (adj.) _____
- watchful keeping; charge; care (noun) _____
- worthless or useless; waste; trash (noun) _____
- living forever; never dying (adj.) _____
- to seek information or advice from; exchange ideas (verb) _____
- troubled; worried; uneasy (adj.) _____

Name _____

TALES OF A FOURTH GRADE NOTHING

ACROSS

1. Peter called Fudge this after he swallowed his two front teeth!
4. Peter got to ride in one after Fudge ate his turtle!
5. Mr. Hatcher made a mushroom _____ with a dozen eggs. It was gross!
8. Fudge rode a toddle-bike in the _____.
12. The author of this and many, many other very creative books! (2 words)
14. Fudgie threw it all over the theater.
16. Peter's name for his new dog.

DOWN

1. Fudge's real first name.
2. Peter's and Fudge's last name.
3. Peter learned to stand on his _____ in gym class. He helped Fudge eat because of it!
6. Baby talk for a sore.
7. Peter's best friend.
9. Peter's grade in school.
10. "Eat it or _____ _____."
11. Fudge should feel lucky that his parents don't believe in this form of discipline.
13. Peter's turtle.
15. Fudge and Peter live in this city.

Name _____

TALES OF A FOURTH GRADE NOTHING

N	B	A	J	Y	C	V	X	K	S	E	Y	Z	C	T
K	D	A	D	S	I	W	E	I	K	X	I	B	L	T
I	Y	X	B	N	P	W	T	O	H	C	L	U	K	H
U	Z	U	N	B	U	O	T	O	O	C	S	S	H	J
F	G	U	D	H	L	G	L	M	M	N	H	Q	F	A
E	K	E	U	E	N	E	M	L	I	R	J	N	B	X
N	Q	N	L	Y	N	I	Q	N	U	T	V	S	S	Y
O	H	B	Y	T	T	L	P	L	A	T	X	G	X	M
X	J	Q	A	T	A	O	Z	O	D	U	I	B	G	Q
L	Z	Q	E	I	L	B	I	H	Q	E	G	O	X	A
Y	H	E	C	I	V	Y	S	U	V	A	G	H	N	D
V	L	E	T	N	N	Z	T	J	G	G	T	G	T	Y
T	P	E	I	K	F	C	N	V	S	T	K	Z	U	Y
S	P	E	R	O	X	I	D	E	S	S	E	Q	M	M
U	Z	S	R	M	X	C	E	C	N	E	I	T	A	P

Directions:

Fill in each blank space below using the vocabulary words in the box. Then find the words in the word search puzzle.

babble	polite	mugged	pollution	peroxide
insult	patience	naughty	special	committee

- more than ordinary; unusual; exceptional (adj.) _____
- bad; not obedient (adj.) _____
- having or showing good manners; behaving properly (adj.) _____
- to have attacked a person from behind, usually to rob (verb) _____
- liquid often used on cuts or scrapes (noun) _____
- group of persons appointed to do some special thing (noun) _____
- to say or do something that hurts someone's feelings (verb) _____
- calm endurance of anything that annoys, troubles, or hurts (noun) _____
- talk that cannot be understood; baby talk (noun) _____
- wastes and poisons (noun) _____

TRAPPED IN DEATH CAVE

ACROSS

7. Death Cave was filled with these. They killed Odie.

10. Mrs. Becker's husband was shot in the back while he was ____.

11. The sheriff of Medicine Park, and a murderer as well!

12. It was thought that Gary's grandpa died because of a _____ accident.

14. Mrs. Becker hot-wired it!

15. Gary called Brian this and then they got into a big, stinky fight!

16. Mrs. Becker's husband.

17. Brian, Gary, and Mrs. Becker were trapped here, inside Death Cave!

DOWN

1. The fishing bait Gary's grandpa often used. (Hint: It didn't smell too good!) (2 words)

2. A small white one bit Gary right on the bottom. Ouch!

3. Another name for a pile of bones.

4. Brian's best friend.

5. Some of the youngsters in town thought Mrs. Becker was one. But not anymore!

6. The author of this thrilling book! (2 words)

8. The Indians who "danced" in the cave. (2 words)

9. One of Odie's occupations.

13. His family often took vacations in Medicine Park.

TRAPPED IN DEATH CAVE

G	W	N	K	B	Q	I	M	L	T	P	K	U	X	B
W	R	U	F	A	X	X	G	N	E	R	R	H	A	R
S	S	E	Y	E	O	U	E	S	E	F	R	W	E	N
X	T	J	E	F	O	I	T	W	U	C	Y	F	I	D
R	W	A	G	D	C	E	E	R	J	C	M	B	H	T
C	J	O	R	N	R	S	G	T	Y	C	X	W	I	J
E	F	J	A	R	F	S	J	L	M	R	R	B	I	G
X	Q	B	O	D	O	U	P	C	H	F	T	I	P	T
W	T	Z	I	P	S	W	N	R	O	X	K	U	W	O
S	R	M	I	V	L	N	H	E	Y	U	J	G	N	A
F	J	G	H	F	D	B	X	E	R	M	E	Y	Z	W
K	E	C	I	Y	C	Y	R	B	A	A	H	G	A	W
G	P	W	F	Z	L	R	I	D	P	D	L	P	Z	J
L	A	N	T	E	R	N	R	M	B	W	E	J	V	C
O	M	I	N	O	U	S	J	Y	I	M	Z	N	X	P

Directions:

Fill in each blank space below using the vocabulary words in the box. Then find the words in the word search puzzle.

sewer	funeral	arrowhead	lantern	spry
pester	ominous	greed	ancient	dim

- belonging to times long past; very old (adj.)   _____
- annoy; trouble; vex (verb)   _____
- active; lively; nimble (adj.)   _____
- tip of an arrow, often made of flint (noun)   _____
- underground pipe for carrying off waste water and refuse (noun)   _____
- case to protect a light from wind or rain (noun)   _____
- ceremony held for a person who is dead (noun)   _____
- of or like a bad omen; unfavorable; threatening (adj.)   _____
- not bright or clear (adj.)   _____
- condition of wanting more than your share (noun)   _____

Name _____

TUCK EVERLASTING

ACROSS

1. She killed the man in the yellow suit, though she really didn't seem like the murdering type!
3. Some hunters shot it clean through, but nothing happened to it!
5. Winnie lived in a "touch-me-not" one.
8. The title of this wonderfully written book! (2 words)
12. Tuck's first name.
13. Winnie poured the magic water on this animal.
14. The whole experience probably changed her life the most.
15. The nearby town where Mae nearly faced the gallows.

DOWN

1. He had two kids.
2. Winnie's last name.
4. The author of *Tuck Everlasting*. (2 words)
5. This animal didn't drink the water, so it died.
6. He asked Winnie to drink the magic water once she turned seventeen.
7. Pancakes.
9. He arrested Mae for killing the man in the yellow suit.
10. Jesse's age at the time he drank the water.
11. If convicted, Mae would have to go to the _____; then everyone would know she couldn't die!

Name _____

TUCK EVERLASTING

D	C	Y	E	N	K	R	K	H	A	S	U	S	P	C
T	C	S	Y	Q	H	H	O	G	S	X	K	S	R	O
M	S	N	C	S	W	B	L	V	A	C	P	B	E	T
F	V	D	J	L	Z	K	D	C	A	C	R	U	C	T
S	Y	J	W	R	A	I	O	J	Q	E	O	L	I	A
J	X	F	W	Q	R	N	P	A	G	X	T	O	O	G
E	O	O	Z	C	S	A	K	A	E	O	E	B	U	E
S	N	H	A	T	L	Y	K	Q	G	F	S	K	S	U
R	B	T	A	F	N	E	Y	Y	E	D	T	S	E	D
E	Y	B	R	M	X	R	O	H	N	F	W	W	X	B
N	L	S	H	A	O	D	S	Q	P	W	J	O	P	W
E	D	Y	L	Q	N	D	I	C	T	Z	L	L	A	Y
F	C	K	A	Y	R	C	S	M	Y	B	Z	L	B	J
F	R	B	V	E	G	K	E	I	I	L	T	A	Y	D
I	J	V	M	E	V	H	F	D	W	T	N	G	W	J

Directions:

Fill in each blank space below using the vocabulary words in the box. Then find the words in the word search puzzle.

acrid	constable	cottage	entranced	flapjacks
gallows	precious	protest	timid	wisdom

- something that is valuable, esteemed, or cherished (adj.) _____
- pancakes (noun) _____
- sharp or harsh (adj.) _____
- having a great understanding of what is true or right (noun) _____
- being hesitant, fearful, or shy (adj.) _____
- a peace officer, like a sheriff, who can make arrests (noun) _____
- small house (noun) _____
- device used for hanging (noun) _____
- to object or disagree (verb) _____
- to be filled with great pleasure, wonder, or enchantment (verb) _____

DISCUSSION QUESTIONS

Banner in the Sky
by James Ramsey Ullman

- Why was Rudi so determined to climb the Citadel?
- Franz and Captain Winter were the first to reach the top of the Citadel. Explain whether or not you think this was fair. Should Rudi have been the first to reach the top? Tell why or why not.
- In the end, Rudi's mother and his Uncle Franz changed their minds about Rudi becoming a guide. What made them change their minds?

The Best Christmas Pageant Ever
by Barbara Robinson

- What do you think caused the Herdmans to take the Christmas pageant so seriously?
- Why did the Herdmans leave their Christmas ham at the pageant?
- In your opinion, were the Herdmans bad people? Defend your answer.

Bunnicula
by Deborah and James Howe

- Why were Chester and Harold so determined to warn their family about Bunnicula?
- If you could have any pet you wanted, what kind would you prefer? List the pros and cons of having that kind of pet.
- Have you ever been suspicious of someone because they acted strangely? Describe the situation, and tell whether or not your suspicions were correct.

The Castle in the Attic
by Elizabeth Winthrop

- Why did William shrink Mrs. Phillips?
- In what ways did William's experiences change his life?
- If you could go on an adventure anywhere you wanted, where would you go? What do you think you would you do there? How long would you stay?

Danny the Champion of the World
by Roald Dahl

- Do you believe Danny and his father were good friends? Defend your answer.
- Danny and his father poached pheasants from Mr. Hazell's woods. Should they have done this? Discuss your opinion.
- How did Danny earn the title of "Champion of the World"?
- Were Danny and his father happy? What makes you think so?

Dear Mr. Henshaw
by Beverly Cleary

- Throughout the book, Leigh had different feelings about his dad. What caused Leigh's feelings to change? Have you ever felt this way?
- At the end of the book, Leigh said that he felt bad and a whole lot better at the same time. How can that be possible? Use an example from your own life.
- If you were to write a letter to any author you chose, who would you write to? Give at least two reasons why you chose that author.

Dunc Breaks the Record
by Gary Paulsen

- Why did Amos choose to go hang gliding with Dunc when he was extremely scared of doing it?
- Why did Milt give Dunc and Amos a bar of gold?
- How did Amos feel about Melissa Hansen?

Hang Tough, Paul Mather
by Alfred Slote

- If you knew Paul Mather, do you think you'd be friends? Justify your answer.
- Why did Paul choose to pitch when he knew it could make him so sick?
- Paul's brother knew he was playing baseball. Why didn't he tell on Paul? Do you think he should have? What would you have done?

Harriet the Spy
by Louise Fitzhugh

- Why were Harriet's friends mad after they read her notebook? If you were one of Harriet's friends, what would you have done?
- Why was Harriet so upset when Ole Golly moved away?
- Describe how you think Harriet felt about her parents.
- Compare the book *Harriet the Spy* to the movie "Harriet the Spy." Which did you enjoy more? Were the characters in the movie like you pictured them while you were reading the book?

Hatchet
by Gary Paulsen

- Was Brian ever worried that he wouldn't survive in the wilderness? Give examples to support your answer.
- In what ways do you think Brian's experiences changed him?
- Which of Brian's many challenges do you believe was the hardest?

How to Eat Fried Worms
by Thomas Rockwell

- What is the grossest thing you've ever eaten? Why did you eat it?
- Do you think Billy should have made the bet and eaten the worms?
- What would you have done if you were in Billy's shoes? Would you have accepted the bet? List at least three reasons why or why not.

The Indian in the Cupboard
by Lynne Reid Banks

- How did Omri's feelings towards Little Bear change as he grew to know Little Bear better?
- How did Omri feel when Little Bear and Boone were sent away?
- If you had a magic cupboard like Omri's, would you use it? If not, share your reasons. If yes, what would you use it for?

Island of the Blue Dolphins
by Scott O'Dell

- Why did Karana risk her life to go back to the island?
- Karana left the island once, in a canoe, but she returned. Why didn't she leave again?
- How was it possible for Karana to become friends with an Aleut girl? After all, the Aleuts killed many of her people.
- In the end, why did Karana decide to leave the island?

James and the Giant Peach
by Roald Dahl

- Compare James's life in the peach to his life with his hideous aunts.
- Is James a hero? List at least three reasons why he was or wasn't one.
- Who was your favorite character in this book? Share the reasons why the character appealed to you so much.

The Lion, the Witch and the Wardrobe
by C.S. Lewis

- Why was Aslan willing to give his life for Edmund?
- What do you think Edumund might say if he knew what Aslan had done for him? What would you say if you were Edmund?
- Do you think Peter, Susan, Edmund, and Lucy were glad to come back to our world, or do you feel they may have been happier in Narnia?
- Do you see any similarities between the professor and Aslan? Explain your answer.

Matilda
by Roald Dahl

- Of all the tricks Matilda played on people, which was your favorite?
- Why do you think Matilda protected her parents from the FBI?
- Did the Trunchbull get what she deserved? Explain your answer.
- In the end, where do you think the Trunchbull went?

Mr. Popper's Penguins
by Richard and Florence Atwater

- How was Mr. Popper able to keep the penguins alive out of their natural environment?
- Do you feel Mr. Popper made the right decision when he chose to free the penguins rather than use them to make money? What would you have done in his situation?
- Think of some animals and their natural habitats. Imagine what would happen in your house if one of those animals arrived on your doorstep. Describe how you would cope with the surprise, and what adjustments you would have to make.

My Side of the Mountain
by Jean Craighead George

- Why did Sam leave his home to go live off the land?
- How did Sam's parents feel about his leaving?
- Do you think Sam was ever lonely? Explain your answer.
- In the end, Sam's family joins him! How do you feel about this ending? Would you change the ending in any way? Tell how.

Sarah, Plain and Tall
by Patricia MacLachlan

- How did Caleb and Anna feel about Sarah?
- Why do you think Sarah chose to stay with Caleb and Anna instead of returning home?
- Would you like to live the way Caleb and Anna lived? Share your decision.

Shiloh
by Phyllis Reynolds Naylor

- As you know, Marty kept Shiloh a secret for quite a while. Do you believe it was all right for Marty to do this? What would you have done?
- What do you think Marty would have done if Judd had misled him and kept Shiloh?
- Have you ever had, or do you have, a pet that you've cared about as much as Marty cared about Shiloh? Describe your pet and what makes it so special to you.

The Sign of the Beaver
by Elizabeth George Speare

- Name at least three survival techniques that Attean taught Matt.

- How did Matt's attitude change towards Indians after he got to know Attean?
- How did Attean's attitude change towards white men after getting to know Matt?
- Matt chose not to leave with Attean and his people. What would you have done if you were Matt?

Strider
by Beverly Cleary

- In what ways did Strider help Leigh?
- Why do you think Leigh kept a diary?
- Describe how Leigh has changed since **Dear Mr. Henshaw**?

Tales of a Fourth Grade Nothing
by Judy Blume

- What would you do if you were Peter and had a brother like Fudge?
- In your opinion, what was the worst thing Fudge did?
- Do you think Peter's feelings towards Fudge changed once Peter had a dog?

Trapped in Death Cave
by Bill Wallace

- Have you ever fought with your best friend, like Brian and Gary did? If so, how did you feel afterwards? How can friends avoid getting into fights?
- Why do you think Mrs. Becker was willing to accompany Brian up to Death Cave? After all, she said she wouldn't go there for a million dollars!
- Which part of the book did you consider the most exciting?

Tuck Everlasting
by Natalie Babbitt

- Why do you think Winnie decided not to drink the water? Discuss what you would have done.
- How do you think Jesse felt about Winnie not drinking the water?
- As you know, Mae killed the man in the yellow suit. Does that make her a criminal? What do you think should happen to her?
- Were the Tucks happy people? Explain your answer.

ANSWERS

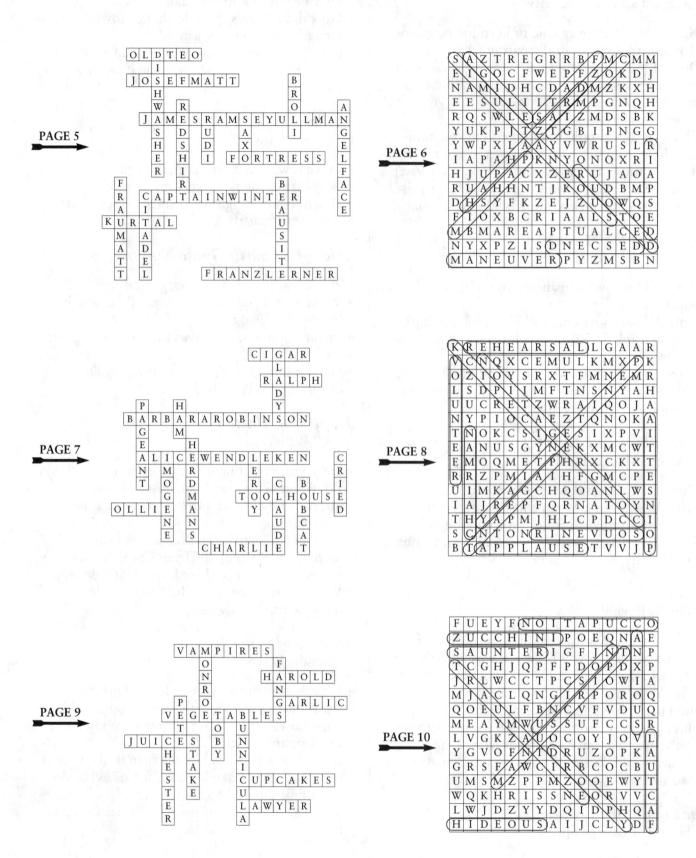

PAGE 5

PAGE 6

PAGE 7

PAGE 8

PAGE 9

PAGE 10

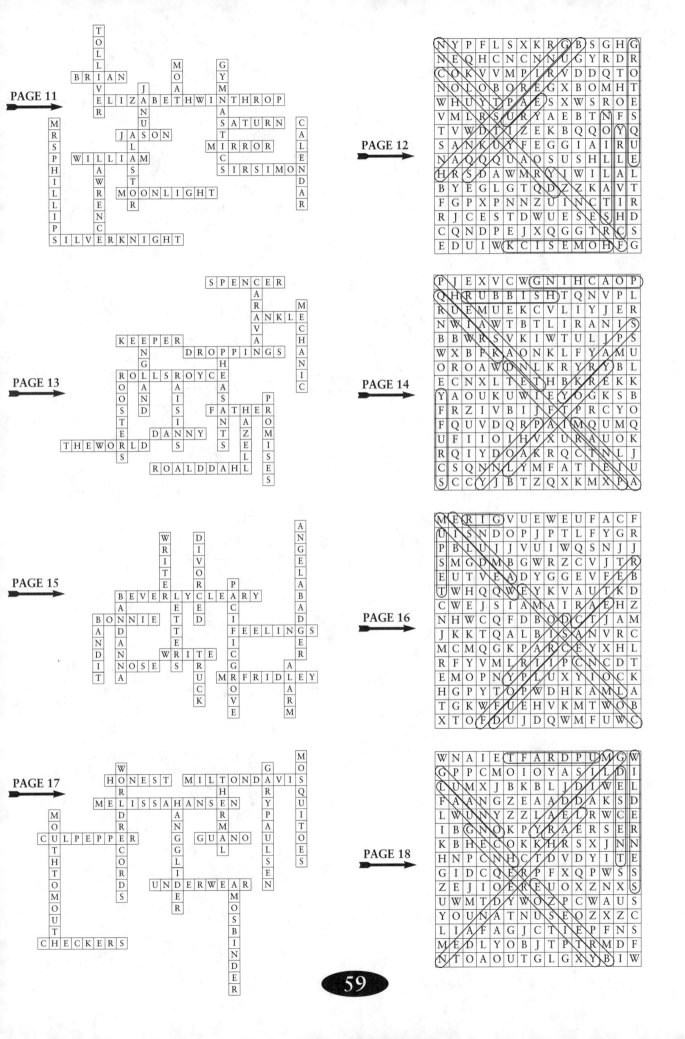

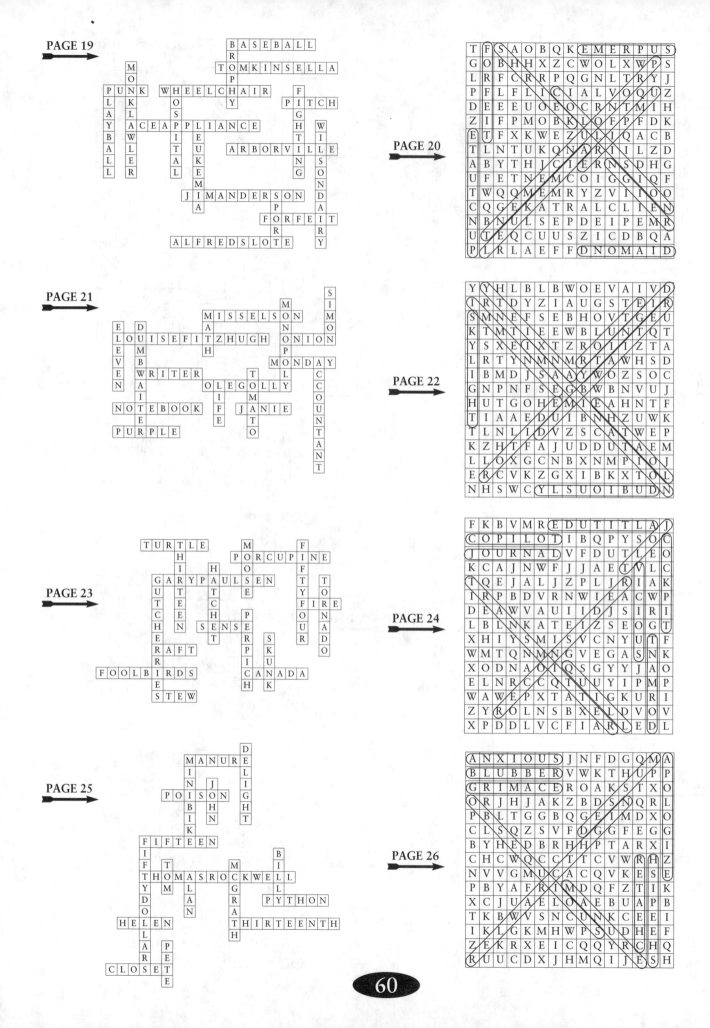

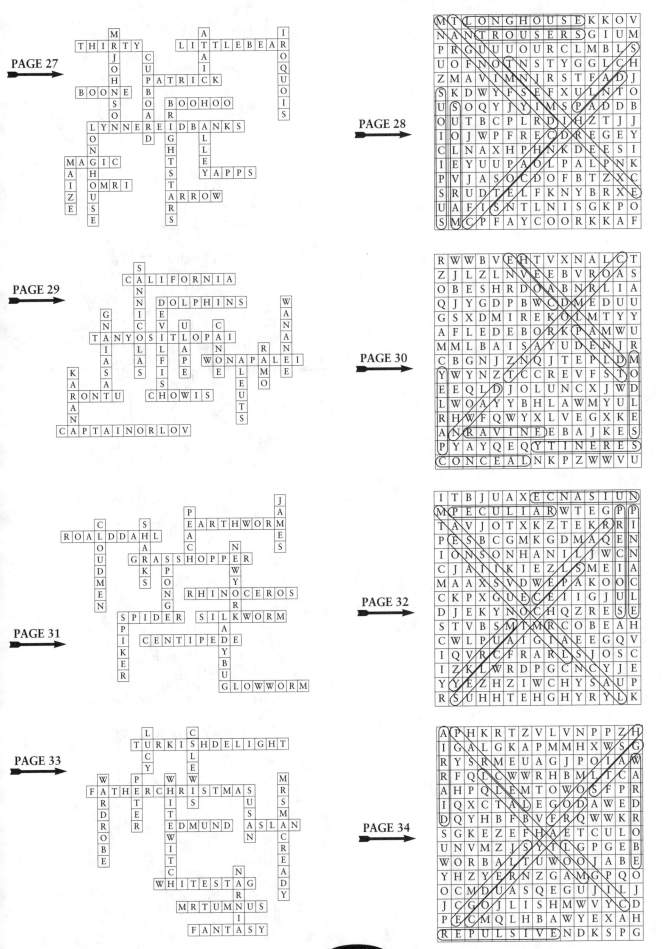

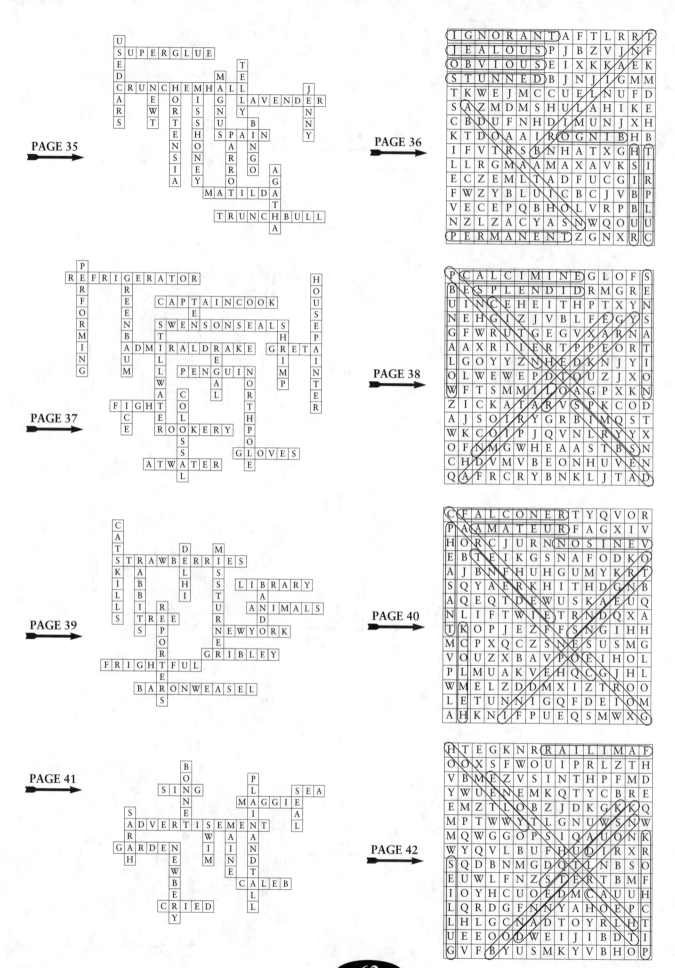

PAGE 35 ➜

PAGE 36 ➜

PAGE 37 ➜

PAGE 38 ➜

PAGE 39 ➜

PAGE 40 ➜

PAGE 41 ➜

PAGE 42 ➜

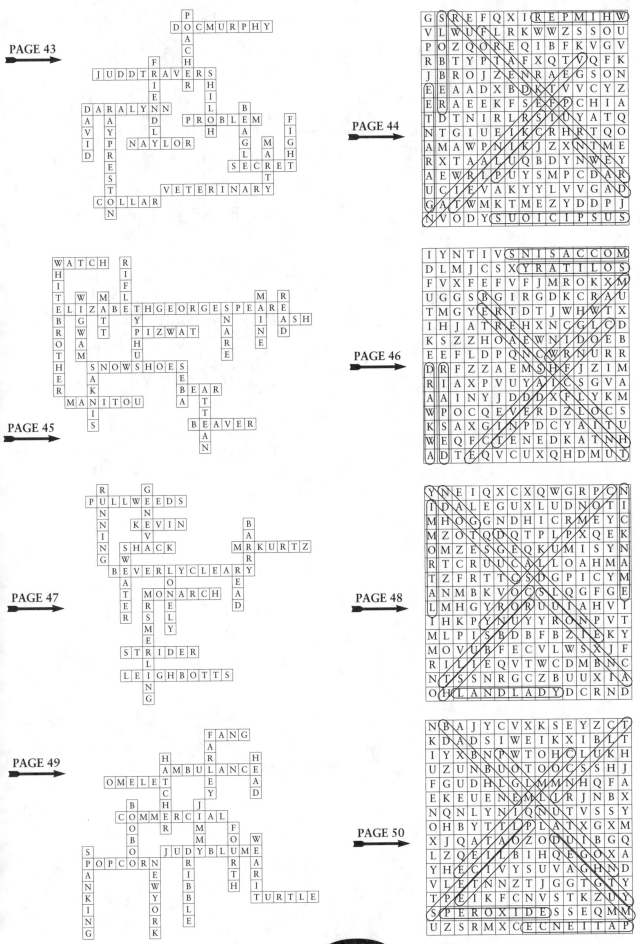

PAGE 43
PAGE 44
PAGE 45
PAGE 46
PAGE 47
PAGE 48
PAGE 49
PAGE 50

PAGE 51 →

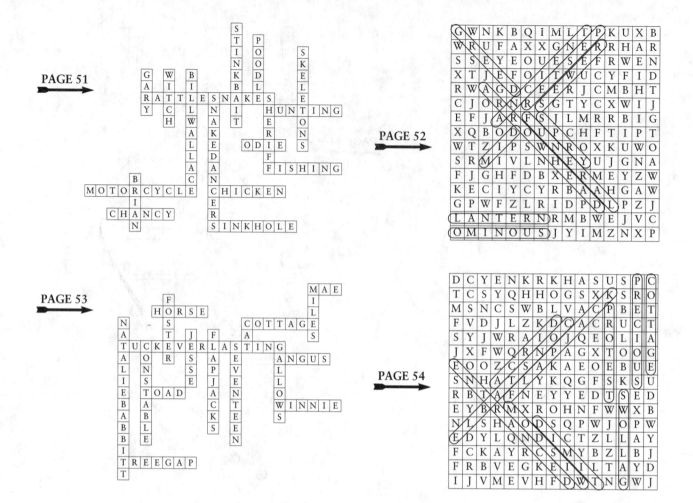

PAGE 52 →

PAGE 53 →

PAGE 54 →